PAN AMERICAN FLIGHT #863

to Paradise!

From the author's small town of Panganiban to the vast plains of America, including collection of inspirational poems & other literary works.

(Sequel to the "The Thing of Beauty is a Joy Forever")

V O L U M E   I I

FRANK A. DE LA ROSA

The Holy Bible, English Standard Version. ESV® Text
Edition: 2016. Copyright © 2001 by Crossway Bibles,
a publishing ministry of Good News Publishers.

To order additional copies of this book, contact:
Xlibris
1-888-795-4274
www.Xlibris.com
Orders@Xlibris.com

ISBN: Softcover   978-1-7960-7252-5
         EBook   978-1-7960-7251-8

Print information available on the last page

Rev. date: 04/07/2020

This book is printed in United States of America.

Other Books of Mr. De La Rosa:
1.) A Touch of Life
2.) The Thing of Beauty is a Joy Forever
3.) Pan American Flight #863 to Paradise! 3 Volumes

DEAR LORD

Dear lord, thank you for helping us survive this year full of struggles. We look forward that you'll be giving us another year, a great chance to try again for the good of us all. Please light our path and guide us all along.

We need Your help, Lord, as we try to navigate and explore the course of so many changes and challenges ahead of us. But, lord, we are tired as the results of the ups and downs of our nation's economy and the so many other things which are affecting our lives here and abroad. We're so much overwhelmed of what the future may bring to all of us and the coming generations. Lord,give us courage and strength to carry on. Our hope and trust are in You.

Open our eyes to small things. No matter how good our vision, help us that our hearts will probe deeper. Let there be silence, so that we may hear Your voice when You talk to us in the quietness of our mind. Give us strength and hope as we search out within ourselves and in some small corners of the world in which we can serve others. Sharpen our intellects and our awareness. Help us ponder into the wonderment of our existence, building bridges to the unforeseeable future of this year, leaving a legacy for those who come behind us.

Get us up, Lord, when we falter. Give us the faith and the strength to begin each day anew in the service of our families, our friends, our community, our church and above all to You. let us so lived that when this year is finished, we are happy to say, that we have lived life to its fullest, that is by living life, one day at a time. All praise, honor, and glory be to God forever and ever. Amen.

This book is lovingly dedicated
to Joy, my youngest daughter and
her husband Raymond Monzon and their
3 children Nico, Sara and Luke.

Having fun with my new cowboy hat & tie.

Last Respects To Share With You

One day not too long ago, the employees of a large company in St. Louis, Missouri returned from their lunch break and were greeted with a sign on the front door. The sign said: "Yesterday the person who has been hindering your growth in this company passed away. We invite you to join the funeral in the room that has been prepared in the gym." At first everyone was sad to hear that one of their colleagues had died, but after a while they started getting curious about who this person might be. The excitement grew as the employees arrived at the gym to pay that last respects. Everyone wondered: "Who is this person who was hindering my progress? Well, at least he is no longer here!"

One by one the employees got closer to the coffin and when they looked inside it they suddenly became speechless. They stood over the coffin, shocked and in silence, as if someone had touched the deepest part of their soul.

There was a mirror inside the coffin: everyone who looked inside it could see himself. There was also a sign next to the mirror that said: "There is only one person who is capable to set limits to your growth: it is YOU."

You are the only person who can revolutionize your life. You are the only person who can help yourself. Your life doesn't change when your boss changes, when your friends change, when your parents change, when your partner changes, when your company changes. Your life changes when You change, when you go beyond your limiting beliefs, when you realize that you are the only one responsible for your life.

Aerial view of my second hometown, San Francisco California.

This is one of my favorite plants in in our garden. Best for suman flavoring...PANDAN PALM.

Please help me. What kind of a flower is this?

Our high-towering Avocado Trees.

Last Calamansi fruits left for Winter.

MORINGA: The Powerful Malunggay Tree at its best!

What a beautiful morning!

Let's break the chilly morning with a hot cup of coffee! Happy Advent Season my FB friends!

(Second Caribbean Cruise, 2015)

Top of Giant Papaya Tree! Amazing! Frutis never get ripen!

Relaxing...
@ Melbourne Square Mall

Relaxing...on free days at MELBOURNE SQUARE MALL. So nice a place to be.

LOVE OF GOD AND LOVE OF COUNTRY

Patriotism takes many forms and is strengthened and expressed in a variety of ways. Love of God and love of country have been integral concepts of our people since the founding of our nation. Our forefathers believed in those principles and laid the cornerstone for all future generations' freedoms by punctuating the pages of history with the rights of the individual to love of God and country. Of such vital importance were these truths that they were declared as being "self evident" by the writers of our Declaration of Independence.

The sight of our country's flag unfurled and flying in the breeze, a stirring rendition of the Star Spangled Banner, the Pledge of Allegiance delivered with feeling - all evoke a deepening of our patriotic pride.

Who among us has not had at least one tear come to our eyes, or placed our hand over our heart, or had our emotions swell with pride as we watched a military parade composed of divisions of uniformed representatives, male and female, of all branches of the service, groups of veterans of all ages and wars, and members of various auxiliaries marching in step to the roll of the drums?

The privileges and rights we enjoy today were made possible by the sacrifices of our forefathers and men and women whose dedication to God and our country prevailed through those turbulent years. Let's then reaffirm our commitment to maintain the freedoms on which our country was founded and to work for peace in our troubled world. God Bless America!

"Enjoying a Tricycle Ride!"

Oh, yes! It's fun to have a Tricycle Ride...somewhere in the wonderland...Cozumel City, Mexico.

Walking down the busy street of the world...Cozumel City, Mexico.

IN JOINING THE KNIGHTS OF COLUMBUS

For over fifty years ago, while I was growing up in the Philippines - living in a small town of approximately 9,000 people, it never occurred in my mind that the Knights of Columbus existed in the Philippines. Should I have the opportunity to know it, the chance was that I could never belong to it. The truth was that only the well-to-do families, the public officials, and the elite group were at their best interest to join this fraternal organization. Considering the situation in an economic perspective I came to believe why this was so. And besides, it's only in the capital and big cities that they organized this Knights of Columbus. It was really a blessing for me to find myself in the sunshine state called Florida, where I found the opportunity to be a member of the Knights of Columbus since 1994. This makes a whole new world of difference for me all along.

For all Catholic men, 18 years and older, and who are interested in joining the Knights of Columbus, please allow me to tell you some interesting things that I know about the Knights of Columbus.

The Knights of Columbus is the world's largest family, fraternal, service organization with 1.8 million members, that's covering the United States, Canada, the Philippines, Mexico, Puerto Rico, Cuba, Dominican Republic, Guam, Panama, the Virgin Islands, and the Bahamas. It provides members and their families with volunteer opportunities in service to the Catholic Church, their communities, families, and young people.

As a knight, imagine as being part of an organization that fills your heart and your mind with the joy of giving to others and the feeling of satisfaction that comes with making a difference in touching other people's lives. The members are men committed to making their community a better place, while supporting their church. Being a knight is more than a camaraderie, it is being involved with your community; it's supporting your local church, while enhancing your own faith and family life, and protecting life - for people who cannot speak for themselves, the born and the unborn.

The Knights of Columbus has four core principles that come in this order: Charity, Unity, Fraternity, and Patriotism. The four degrees of membership come respectively in the same order as the four core principles. The First degree is the first step in becoming a member of this organization. Subsequent degrees & ceremonies are held throughout the year. You are considered a full member ofthe Knights of Columbus once you attained the Third degree.

Once you attained the Third degree membership and in good standing, you are eligible to join the Fourth degree. The Fourth degree imparts a lesson in the virtue of Patriotism. The Fourth degree color guard are the members of Knights of Columbus that you see with regalia (cape, chapeaux, and sword) during parades and other Knights of Columbus ceremonies and activities. As a final note, the Knights of Columbus, as do most Fraternal organizations, keeps the contents of their ceremonials secret..

To be a member, please contact a member of the Knights of Columbus and inquire about joining. If you don't know a member, contact your parish priest or check the phonebook with a local council. If you still are having trouble finding a member, visit the Knights of Columbus web site, www.kofc. org, and use the "Find A Council " feature. Wishing you the best for your search.

"The Beauty of Light"

An ordinary thing around you, can also be extraordinary in the eye of a photographer. -By Paco of Florida.

Anyone knows what kind of a flower is this? Thanks!

A LOVING TRIBUTE TO MY PETS: CHARLIE, ROCKY, SALSA, & RICO.

My Pets in Heaven by Francis dela Rosa

For all the times that you have stooped and touched my head, fed me my favorite treat and returned the love I unconditionally gave to you. For the care that you gave to me unselfishly. For all these things I am grateful and thankful.

I ask that you not to grieve for the loss, but rejoice in the fact that we lived, loved and touched each other lives. My life was fuller because you were there, not as a master/owner, but as my FRIEND.

Today I am as I was in my youth. The grass is always greener, butterflies flit among the flowers and the sun shines gently down upon all of God's creatures. I can run, jump, play, and all of the things that you taught me in my youth. There's no sickness, no aching joints and no regrets and no aging.

We await the arrival of our lifelong companions and know that togetherness is forever. You live in our hearts as we do in yours. Companions such as you are so special! Don't hold the love that you have within yourself. Give it to another like me and then I will live forever. For love never really dies, you are loved and missed as surely as we are.

Here is my favorite garden chair. You are invited to sit and relax on it.

Appetizer at Red Lobster Restaurant in Melbourne Florida.

LETTER FROM HEAVEN TO SHARE WITH MY FRIENDS:

To my beloved husband, Paco of my love, and my dearest family, some things I'd like to say. But first of all, to let you know, that I arrived okay. I'm writing this letter from heaven and I dwell with God above. Here, there's no more tears of sadness; but just eternal peace, happiness and love.

Please do not be unhappy just because I am out of sight. Remember that I am with you every morning, noon and night. That day I had to leave you when my life on earth was through. God picked me up and hugged me and He said, "I welcome you;

It's good to have you back again, you were missed while you were gone. As for your dearest family, they will be here later on. I need you here badly, you're a part of my plan.
There's so much that we have to do, to help our mortal man."

God gave me the list of things, that He wished for me to do. And the foremost on the list, was to watch and care for you. And when you lie in bed at night the day's chores put to flight. God and I are closest to you... in the middle of the night.

When you think of my life on earth, and all those loving years. Because you are only human, they are bound to bring you tears. But do not be afraid to cry: it does relieve the pain.
Remember there would be no flowers, unless there was some rain.

I wish that I could tell you all that God has planned.
If I were to tell you, you wouldn't understand.
But one thing is for certain, though my life on earth is over. I'm closer to you now, than I ever was before.

There are many rocky roads ahead of you and many hills to climb;
But together we can do it by taking one day at a time.
It was always in my mind and I'd like it for you too;
That as you give unto the world, the world will give to you.

If you can help somebody who is in sorrow and pain; Then you can say to God at night...
"My day was not in vain."
And now I am contented...that my life was worthwhile.
Knowing as I passed along the way I made somebody smile.

So if you meet somebody who is sad and feeling low; Just lend a hand to pick him up, as on your way you go.
When you're walking down the street and you've got me on your mind;
I'm walking in your footsteps only half a step behind.

And when it's time for you to go... from your body to be free. Remember you're not going... you're coming here to me.

Happy New Year Greetings to All!
(2006)

This is our Live 15-ft. Tall Christmas Tree in front of our house. We need help to decorate it this holiday season. Anyone?

Our Gabbie Patch! For Pinangat & Laing (Bicol Express).

Papaya fruits waiting to be harvested before the cold spill in Florida. I'm making some Atsara to share with friends.

Greetings!

Happy Thanksgiving to All!

HAPPY THANKSGIVING TO ALL!
(2007)

frank's creation 2009

The Majestic Magnolia!

Frank was a KofC kitchen volunteer.

GOD WORKS IN MYSTERIOUS WAYS

This is a real-life story that I'm going to tell you just happened not too long ago. The memories are still fresh in my mind. My wife and I were on our way to the Philippines to attend the Golden Jubilee Reunion in the high school that I attended, class of '58, in the very remote island in the pacific. Of course the sceneries in the island were so beautiful and very nostalgic, being away for fifty years since our high school graduation.

In the early morning of our fourth day in Manila, I could feel something strange. I didn't know what it was, but I could sense that there was something happening in our room. I don't like to wake up my wife because a day before we were out visiting Holy Shrines in the outskirts of Manila and I knew fully well that she must be very tired. Easter Sunday was just more than a week away, so we still have enough time to have a glimpse of Manila before we proceeded to the island where our reunion was supposed to be. At this point in time, an inner voice told me that I should wake up my wife. My instinct is reliable. So I called her name, but she wasn't responding. I got scared! I felt her pulse at the carotid, pulse point on her neck, and I felt too that she had an elevated temperature. "This was a serious problem," I thought. I called for help, but her brother just left for work earlier. When I got out the garage door, her sister-in-law was just about to leave for work, and coincidentally our service car and the driver just came to pick us up. The timing was just so perfect. Instead of calling an ambulance, our service car driver and my sister-in-law helped me drove my wife to the nearest hospital. My wife's temperature was 104. My wife was confined in the hospital for three days. After she was discharged from the hospital, we rested for a couple of days and then left for the island. I believed that God watches all of His creations every minute of the day and of the night.

I thought that in the meanwhile we won't have problems anymore. However, this wasn't always the case. From Manila, we flew to the island, the capital of the province. From the capital, we rented a service car plus a driver. On our way to my hometown, we have to pass through high mountains, rivers, and beautiful waterfalls. It was really awesome just to look around. When we're about halfway to our destination, at almost top of the mountain, the road on both ways were covered with mud and large rocks, that it was impossible for us to get through. It was Wednesday, just a day before Holy Thursday, and we really wanted to attend the traditional procession of all Saints in our church, to be held in the evening. Life was really full of surprises and mysteries. Honestly, we didn't really know who our town mayor was in my hometown. This was another God 's surprise for us. Our town mayor was also stuck in the mud with us, including the long line of traffic behind us. My nephew told me who the mayor was, and without further ado, I introduced myself to him and we became friends. Without even an introduction, the Mayor seemed to know me so very well. He told me that he already called the highway people, and the mud and the rocks will be cleared away. Instead of waiting for the construction equipments to come, the mayor told us that he already called a service car at his office and it's on its way to pick us up. So with God 's another mysterious ways, our problem solved by itself. My wife and I, and another classmate of mine, also attending the reunion joined us with our mayor on our way to our old home, sweet home.. With God, there's nothing impossible to accomplish. Because of God 's mercy and His infinite wisdom, our vacation and our class reunion ended up beautifully and successfully. He also brought us back to the USA, safe and sound. All praise, honor, and glory be to God, forever and ever. Amen. -By Frank A. De La Rosa

Russian Comfrey Herb in bloom. Looks like Lakad Buran.

Coleus plants sprawling in our yard.

TOGETHER WE CAN MAKE THIS TROUBLED WORLD SMILE!

(A NEW YEAR'S RESOLUTION)

This year I resolved to do my best:

To be so at peace with God, family, friends and the
world around me
that nothing can shake my tranquility.

To speak positively of my physical, spiritual, and
material blessings.

To fmd something good in my friends and tell
them, "You are a very
special person to me."

To look on the brighter side of every dark cloud.

To expect the best of every day, to work for it to
happen,
and to keep my happy thoughts.

To have enthusiasm about life, and to be happy
about the successes of
those around me.

To put the past behind, my mistakes and the
mistakes of others,
and make each stumbling block a stair.

To put on a smile the first thing in the morning
and leave it
in place until I retire at night.

To spend more time in improving myself, like
losing
some weight, rather than criticizing others.

To be so secure to worry, too patient to anger,
too strong
to fear, and too joy-filled to allow a troubled
thought
to cross my horizon.

To spend quality time with my family.
And to continue praying for PEACE in
this so troubled world. Amen.

Donated by Frank and Mary Grace De La Rosa on Mothers Day.

During a Boat Cruise at St. John's River via Barbara Lee's River Paddle Boat in early Spring of 2015.

TOGETHER WE CAN MAKE THIS TROUBLED WORLD SMILE! A NEW YEAR'S PRAYER

Dear Lord, we praise You for the beauty and glory of Christmas season that we just had. We thank you for giving us another year, a chance to try again.

We need Your help Lord, as we try to navigate the course of the so many new challenges ahead of us. But, Lord, we are tired as the results of the ups and down of our nation's economy and other things which are affecting our lives. We're so much worried of what the future may bring to all of us. Lord, give us courage and strength to carry on. Our hope and trust are in you.

Open our eyes to small things. No matter how good our vision, let our hearts probe deeper. Let there be silence so that we may hear Your voice when You talk to us in the quietness of our mind. Give us strength as we search out in some small corners of the world in which we can serve others. Sharpen our intellects and our awareness. Help us ponder into the wonderment of our existence, building bridges to the unforeseeable future of this year, leaving a legacy for those who come behind us.

Get us up, Lord, when we falter. Give us the faith and the strength to begin each day anew in service of our families, our friends, our community, and You. Let's us so lived that when this year is finished we may say, that we have lived a life to its fullest - that is living life one day at a time. All praise, honor, and glory be to God forever and ever. Amen.

HAPPY THOUGHTS TO PONDER

Laughter promotes good health, for body, mind and spirit. It not only brightens your mood but also eases tension. A good dose of laughter has been shown to improve blood circulation, stimulate digestion, lower blood pressure, and prompt the brain to release pain-reducing endorphins.

Laughter is also an expression of faith in God - it is the best response you can make to your own human frailties as you strive to live a happy life.

Driving home after the Saint John's River Cruise.

Peppermint herb for green tea.

Prayer for my friends, relatives & others

Dear Heavenly Father, I ask you to bless my friends, relatives
and those that we're concerned and cared for deeply, who are
reading this prayer right now.

Show them a new revelation of your love and power.
O, Holy Spirit, we ask you to minister to their spirit
at this very moment wherever they are.

Where there is pain, give them your peace and mercy
Where there is self-doubt, release a renewed confidence
through Your grace.
Where there is need, I ask You to fulfill their needs,
like seeking employment, and other
personal needs.

Bless their homes, families, finances, their
goings and their comings.

I ask all these through Jesus Christ, Our Lord
to Whom all good things come.
Amen.

Extra large Upo hanging on the trellis.

A Kayanga (Gumamela) flower in out front yard.

Some Inspirational *Thoughts* to *Ponder:*

Don't go for looks, they can deceive. Don't go for wealth - even that too fades away. Go for someone who makes you smile because only smile makes a dark day bright. There are moments in life when you really miss someone so much that you want to pick them from your dreams and hug them for real.

When one door of happiness closes, another opens but often we look so long at the closed door that we don't see the one which has been opened for us.

The beginning of love is to let those we love be perfectly themselves, and not twist them with our own image - otherwise we love only the reflection of ourselves we find in them.

It takes a minute to have a crush on someone, an hour to like someone, and a day to love someone, but it takes a lifetime to forget someone.

Happiness lies for those who cry, those who hurt, those who have searched and who have tried.

A sad thing about life is that sometimes you meet who means a lot to you only to find out in the end that it was never bound to be and you have to let go.

Love starts with a smile, develops with a kiss and ends with a tear.

It hurts to love someone and not to be loved in return, but what is the most painful is to love someone and never finding the courage to let the person know how you feel.

The brightest future will always be based on the brighter past, you can't go on well in life until you let go of your past failures and heartaches.

Never say goodbye when you still want to try - never give up when you still can take it - never say you don't love that person anymore when you can't let go.

When life hands you lemons, make some lemonade...and share with friends.

Giving someone all your love is never an assurance that they'll love you back! Don't expect love in return, just wait for it to grow in their hearts; but if it doesn't, be content that it grew in you.

There are things you love to hear but you would never hear it from that person whom you would like to hear it from, but don't be deaf to hear it from the person who says it with his heart.

When you were born, you were crying and everyone around you was smiling...live your life so that when you die, you're smiling and everyone is crying.

Contentment is not the fulfillment of what you want, it's the realization of how much you already have.

It's true that we don't know what we've got until we lose them, but it's also true that we don't know what we have been missing until it arrives.

The happiest of people don't really have the best of everything, they just make the most of everything that comes along the way.

Keep away from people who belittle your ambitions. Small people always do that, but the really great make you feel that you, too, can become great.

The best and most beautiful things in the world cannot be seen or touched...but are felt in the heart.

When care is pressing you down a bit, rest if you must- but don't quit.

My humble advice is to always, always share your love with your loved ones.

Plant your own garden and decorate your own soul, instead of waiting for someone to bring you flowers.

If we did all the things we were capable of doing, we would literally astound ourselves.

Turn negative attitude into gratitude.

"Katie models in our garden in Palm Bay"

Please meet my imported model from PA.

A flower of Atis (Sugar Apple) fruit tree. Parang Ilang-Ilang flower.

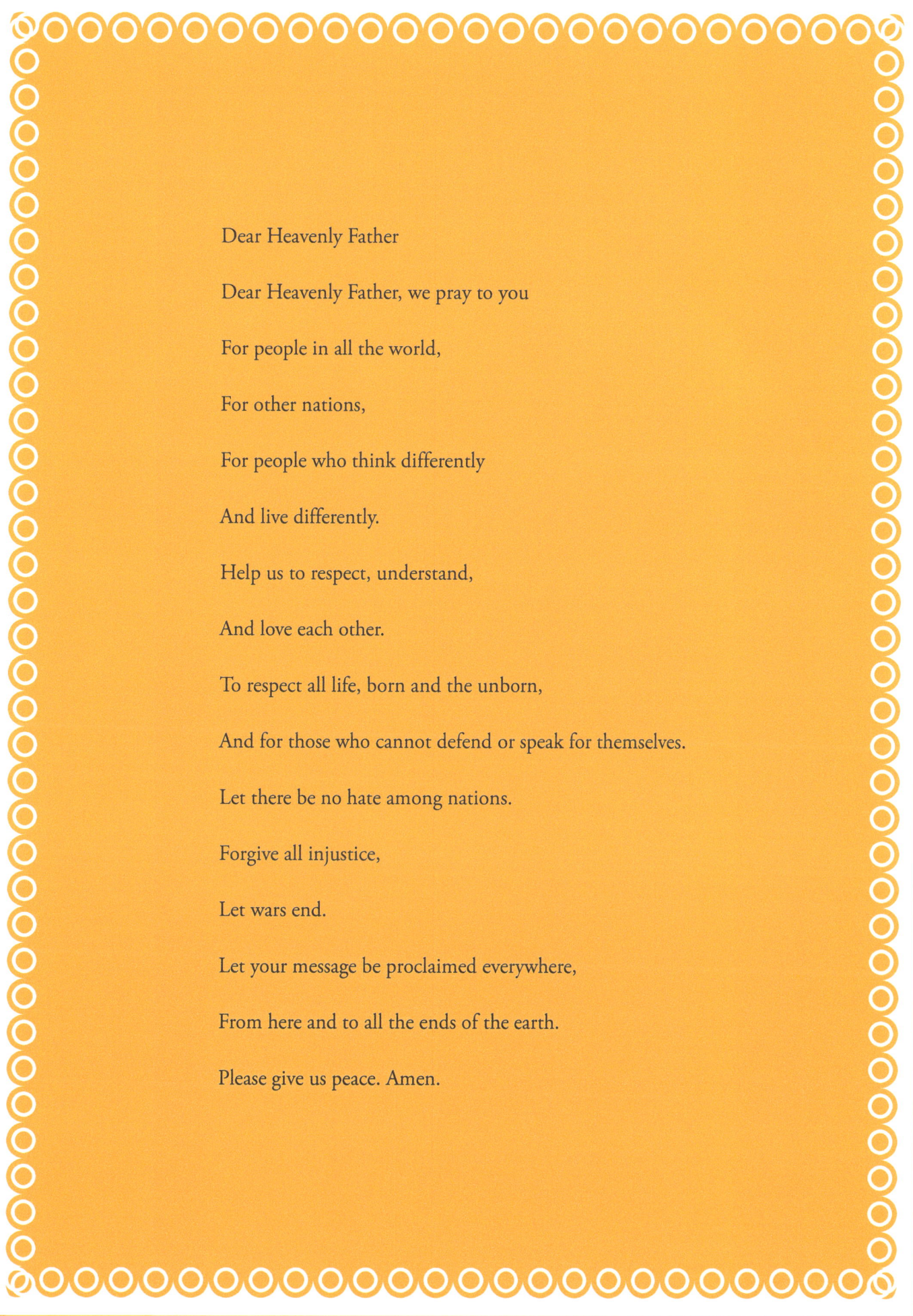

Dear Heavenly Father

Dear Heavenly Father, we pray to you

For people in all the world,

For other nations,

For people who think differently

And live differently.

Help us to respect, understand,

And love each other.

To respect all life, born and the unborn,

And for those who cannot defend or speak for themselves.

Let there be no hate among nations.

Forgive all injustice,

Let wars end.

Let your message be proclaimed everywhere,

From here and to all the ends of the earth.

Please give us peace. Amen.

Friends are the ROSES in life's bouquet.

Rosemary herb in a pot.

Remember That:

Your presence is a gift to the world.
You are unique and one of a kind.
Your life can be what you want to be.
Take the days just one day at a time.

Count your blessings, starting today.
You'll make it through what ever comes along.
Within you are so many answers.
Understand, have courage to be strong.

Do not put limits on yourself.
So many dreams are waiting to be realized.
Love is a journey, not a destination.
Travel its path daily, and your troubles
Will be as fleeting as the footprints in the sand.

Nothing washes more energy than worrying.
The longer one carries a problem, the heavier it gets.
Do not take things so seriously.
Live a life of serenity, not a life of regrets.

Remember that a little good deed goes a long way.
Remember that a lot...goes forever.
Remember that friendship is a wise investment.
Life's treasure are people together.

Realize that it's never too late.
To do ordinary things in an extraordinary way.
Have a happy heart, and hope for the best.
Take the time to wish upon a star.

And don't ever forget...
Even for a day...
How very special person you are!
You are the child of the universe.
And you have the right to be here.

Jackfruit growing from seeds.

An orchid that came along with a "Get Well Card" from a nice couple, Flor & Al. Thanks so very kindly Flor & Al. Surely, it brought sunshine in Room #120 at the rehab center.

GO WITH THE FLOW...LET GO...AND MOVE ON...

Why are some people able to successfully navigate change while others have such a hard time? One of the keys is acceptance.

Resisting change is like rowing against the current. Everything lies there ahead of you. You try to row upstream, back to where you once were.

When you refuse to accept change, you work against the forward momentum taking you to the next phase of your life, and remain stuck in the past.

Every thought that begins with *I can't, I won't or I don't* equals resistance. Argue with reality, and you'll lose every time.

Align your boat with the direction of the river. Stop clinging to the rock, let go of the oars and go with the flow.

On the other side of acceptance is where peace exists, where the solutions are. Draw on your spiritual resources.

Begin to trust, and you can become the person God meant for you become all along.

Saba/Kalibo, another variety of banana.

View in front of our house. This is our home-grown Christmas Tree.

BITS & PIECES:

If God for a second, forgot what I have become and granted me, a little bit to the best of my ability, I wouldn't possibly say everything that is in my mind, but I would be more thoughtful of all I say.

I would give merit to things not for what they are worth, but for what they meant to express. I would sleep little, I would dream more, because I know that every minute we close our eyes, we waste 60 seconds of light. I would walk while others stop. I would awake while others sleep.

If God would give me a little bit more of life, I would dress in a simple manner. I would place myself in front of the sun, leaving not only my body, but my soul naked at its mercy. To the older ones, I would say how mistaken they are when they think they stop falling in love when they grow old, without knowing that they grow old only when they stop falling in love.

I would give wings to children, but I would leave it to them how to fly by themselves. To the elderly, I would say that death doesn't arrive when they grow old, but with forgetfulness.

I have learned so much with all the people I met along life's journey. I have learned that everybody wants to live on top of the mountain, without knowing that true happiness is obtained in the journey taken and the form used to reach the top of the hill. I have learned that when a newborn baby holds, with its little hand, his father's finger, it has trapped him for the rest of his life. I have learned that a man has the right and obligation to look down at another man, only when that man needs help to get up from the ground.

Say always what you feel, not what you think. If I knew that today is the last time I saw you, I would hug you, with all my strength and I would pray to the Lord to let me the guardian angel of your soul. If I knew these are the last moments to see you, I would say "I love you". There is always tomorrow, and life gives us another opportunity to do things right, but in case I am wrong, and today is all that is left to me, I would love to tell you how much I love you and that I will never forget you.

Tomorrow is never guaranteed to anyone, young or old. Today could be the last time to see your loved ones, which is why you must not wait, do it today, in case tomorrow never arrives. I am sure you will be sorry you wasted the opportunity today to give a smile, a hug, a kiss, and that you were too busy to grant them their
last wish.

Keep your loved ones near you, tell them in their ears and to their faces how much you need them and love them. Love them and treat them well; take your time to tell them "I am sorry", "please", "thank you", and all those loving words you know. Ask the Lord for wisdom and strength to express them. Show your friends and loved ones how important they are to you.

Grapes/Obas.

Malunggay (Moringa).

My Christmas List of Blessings

My Christmas List is more than just a way to keep track of the special people God has brought into my life to love and to care for. It's like a treasured family book filled with yesterday's fond memories of all the times God's answered prayer through family and friends.

Every name is a touchstone that leads to a place and time, where God has used another heart to reach out and touch ours. It may have happened some years ago or just yesterday. But every person on my Christmas List has helped me grow and find a way to happiness for me.

So please know that this greeting is more than just a Christmas wish.

It is a "thank you" card to God for putting you on my list. Each and everyone whose name I've come to hold on dear - those who have shown me Christmas joy each day of the year.

Love & Best Wishes
Always, Frank De La Rosa

So vibrant! So radiant! GUMAMELA

Close up of a sweet potato tops.

A cluster of Filipino eggplants in our yard.

A climbing Clematis plant.

Kalachuchi (Plumeria) plant along with sweet potato.

Frank & Grace with Fr. Wilmer Tria of Naga City at the Ina ng Bikol Picnic, Cocoa Beach, FL.

CHRISTMAS: A NATIONAL FIESTA IN THE PHILIPPINES

The Philippines is known as the "Land of Fiestas," and at Christmas time, this is especially true. Filipinos are proud to proclaim their Christmas celebration to be the longest and merriest in the world. It begins formally on December 16 with attendance at the first of nine pre-dawn or early morning masses and continues on nonstop until the first Sunday of January, Feast of the Three Kings, the official end of the season.

The Philippines is the only Asian country where Christians predominate. Majority of the people are Roman Catholic. Christmas, therefore, is an extremely important and revered holiday for most Filipinos. It is a time for family, for sharing, for giving, and a time for food, fun, and friendship.

To most Filipinos, Christmas is the most anticipated fiesta of the year and is celebrated accordingly. The splendid climate of this tropical nation, the abundance and beauty of its flowers, and lovely landscape, its multitude of culinary delights, and above all its warm-hearted people with their true devotion to the family and faith all contribute to a holiday celebrated in the true Philippine fiesta tradition.

FRANK LITO CECILE

GRACE FR. WILMER NELLIE MANNING

A memory to remember by...with good friends.

A banana blossom from our garden (puso ng saging).

A close-up of a Plumeria flower in our yard.

A big banana heart is born in our our garden. A big bunch is coming soon!

Inspirational Passages

I expect to pass this way but once;
any good therefore that I can do,
or any kindness that I can show to
my fellow creature, let me do it now.
Let me not defer it or neglect it,
for I shall not pass this way again.

-Etienne de Grellet

Be at peace with God,
What ever you conceive Him to be,
And whatever your labors and aspirations,
In the noisy confusion of life,
Keep peace with your soul.
With all its sham, drudgery
And broken dreams,
It is still a beautiful world.

-Max Ehrman

Nothing in the world can take the place of persistence.
Talent will not; nothing is more common than unsuccessful
men with talent. Genius will not; unrewarded genius is
almost a proverb. Education will not; the world is full of
educated failures. Persistence and determination alone
are omnipotent.

-Calvin Coolidge

Do it! Move it! Make it happen! No one ever sat their
way to success.

-From Father's Book of Wisdom

Coconut Tree with a bunch of green coconut fruits.

I just loved this painting at the Palm Bay Hospital Main Lobby.

Getting ready to fly to talk to GOD.

Palm Bay, Fl.
June 5, 2015

TBT: This bird greeted me.....HAPPY BIRTHDAY...by our kitchen window. But still...I don't know what kind of bird is this?

Potted sweet potato!

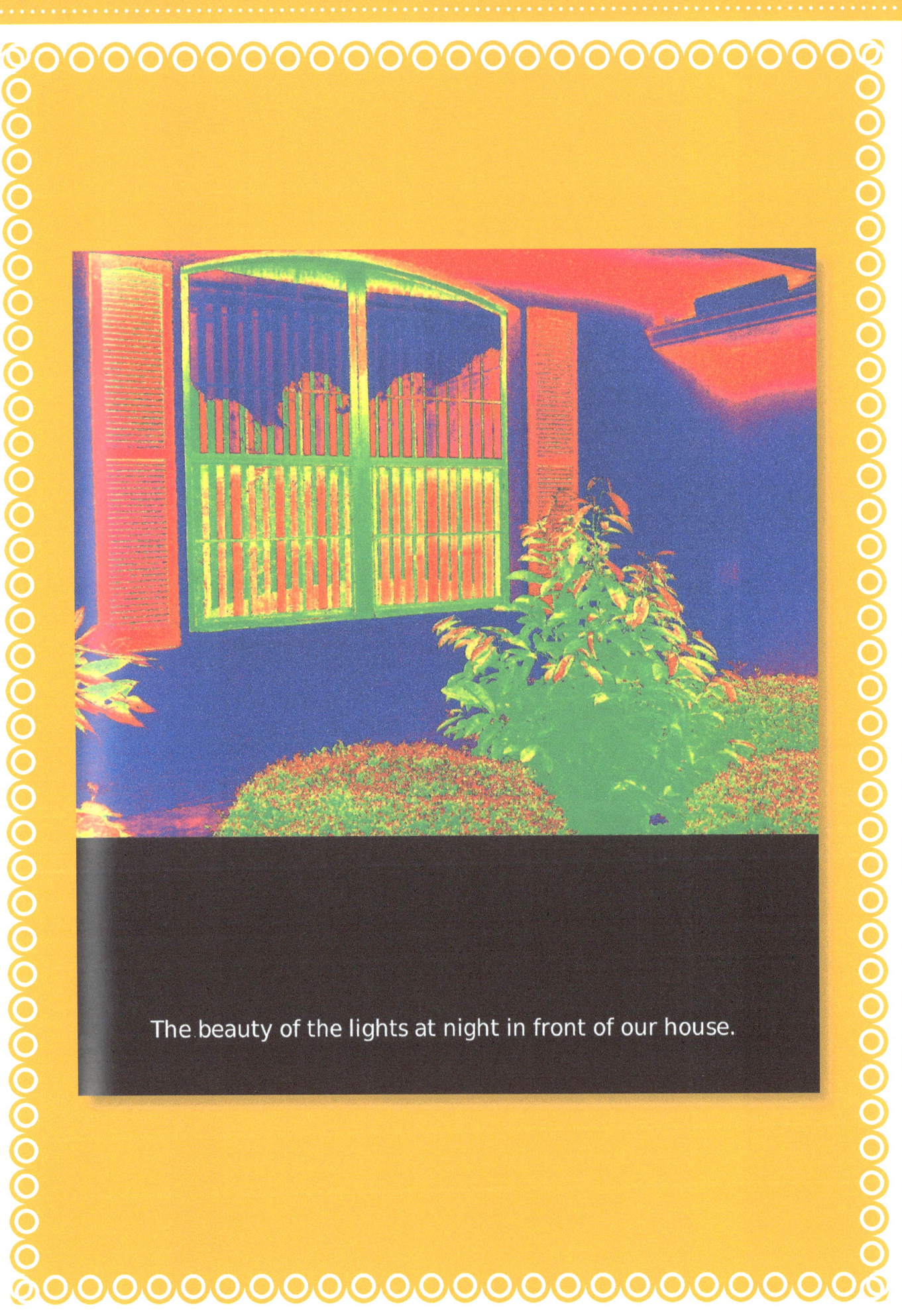

The beauty of the lights at night in front of our house.

Ito nga yung natumbang saba. Bakit kaya natumba?

Birds looking for food in our yard. Are those the carabao's heron?

Saba ready for harvest in our yard.

A RECIPE FOR HAPPINESS

A Recipe For Happiness

4 cups of Love
2 Cups of Loyalty
3 Cups of Forgiveness
1 cup of Friendship
5 Spoons of Hope
4 Quarts of Faith
1 Barrel of Laughter
3 cups of Kindness
2 Cups of Understanding
1 Whole World of Smile
A Whole Lot of Florida Sunshine

Take love and loyalty and mix it with faith. Blend it with tenderness, kindness, understanding, and forgiveness. Add friendship and hope. Sprinkle abundantly with laughter. Bake it with whole lot of Florida Sunshine. Be sure not to overcook it. Serve generously with a big smile!

How to Make Kundol Candy:

Procedure:

Remove the outer green skin of the wintermelon and cut approximately soog winter melon into scm sticks just like potato chips.

Blanched melon by putting into a pot of fresh water with 1tsp of baking soda, and bring to a rapid boil for 1minutes.

Transfer the melon to a colander to drain.

Heat 750g of sugar with 112 Litre of water in a shallow pan until dissolved. Bring the syrup to the boil. Turn down heat to low.

Transfer the drained melon to the pot of syrup.

Press a round of greaseproof paper on top of the melon to immerse the fruit in the syrup.

Bring the syrup slowly to a simmer and simmer for 5 to 10 minutes; do not let it boil.

Take the pan from the heat and allow cooling.

Leave it in the syrup for 24 hours whilst leaving the fruit undisturbed.

Carefully lift the fruit from the syrup and leave to drain for 30 minutes.

Transfer the fruit to paper towels and leave until dry,and store in an airtight container.

Bongolan bananas (another variety of bananas).

Wax Melons (Kondol)
Courtesy of EPCOTT Center, WDW, Orlando Florida

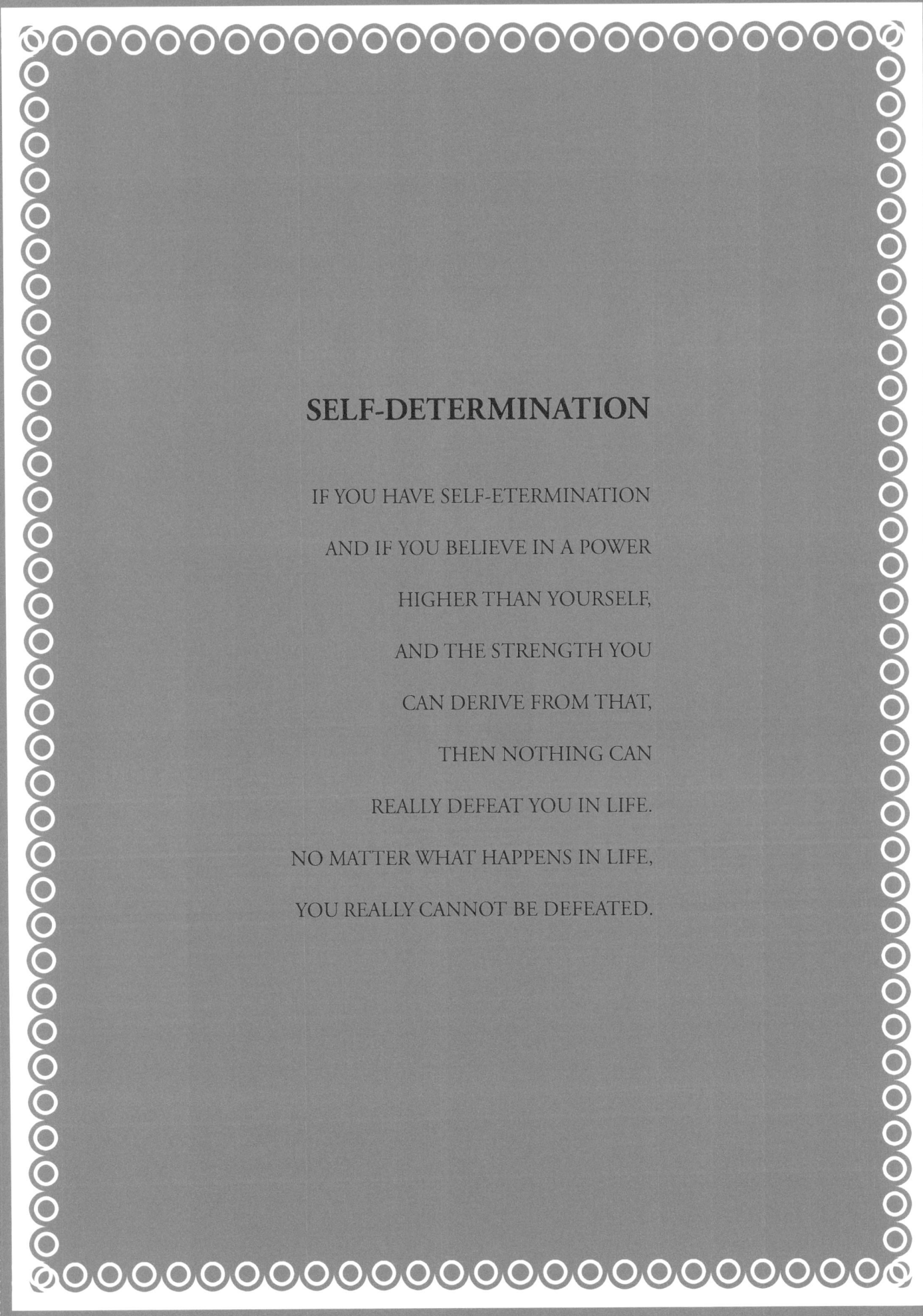

SELF-DETERMINATION

IF YOU HAVE SELF-ETERMINATION

AND IF YOU BELIEVE IN A POWER

HIGHER THAN YOURSELF,

AND THE STRENGTH YOU

CAN DERIVE FROM THAT,

THEN NOTHING CAN

REALLY DEFEAT YOU IN LIFE.

NO MATTER WHAT HAPPENS IN LIFE,

YOU REALLY CANNOT BE DEFEATED.

Animation Resort
Walt Disney World
(2012)

LOW N SLO

A visit to Animation Resort, Walt Disney World...2012!

Kampupot - SAMPAGUITA ng buhay ko!

FAMILY BLESSING

Lord, please bless the family that I love.
And comfort them each day -
As day time turns to night time,
Please bring them peace,
I pray.

When morning comes tomorrow,
Let all their cares be small.
Guide them with Your wisdom -
Lord, bless them one and all.
Amen.

A dream comes true in our own backyard. THE COLOR OF FLORIDA!

Bienvenido...El Cozumel, Mejico! Fun, fun...with the sombrero!

All set for the evening social events.

We're sailing along on the high seas of dreams and memories...

Only God Knows Why?

(A Loving Tribute to my Beloved Mary Grace)

If tears can build a stairway and memories were lane,
I would walk right up to heaven and bring you back again.
No farewell words were spoken and no time to say goodbye,
You were gone before I knew it and only God knows why.
My heart still ache in sadness and secret tears still flow,
What it is meant to lose you no one can ever know.
But now I know you want us to mourn for you no more,
To remember all the happy times we had together,
Life has still much in store.
Since you will never be forgotten,I pledge for you today,
A hallowed place within my heart,is where you'll stay.

A scene viewed at Sanford Downtown, Florida in Spring of 2015.

Mary Grace says:

Hello Everyone!
Thanks all so very much for your kind thoughts and prayers.

A message of thanks from my Mary Grace!

Enjoying the wild St. John River's Boat Ride of Spring.

Autumn Greetings to All!

A postcard from Florida!

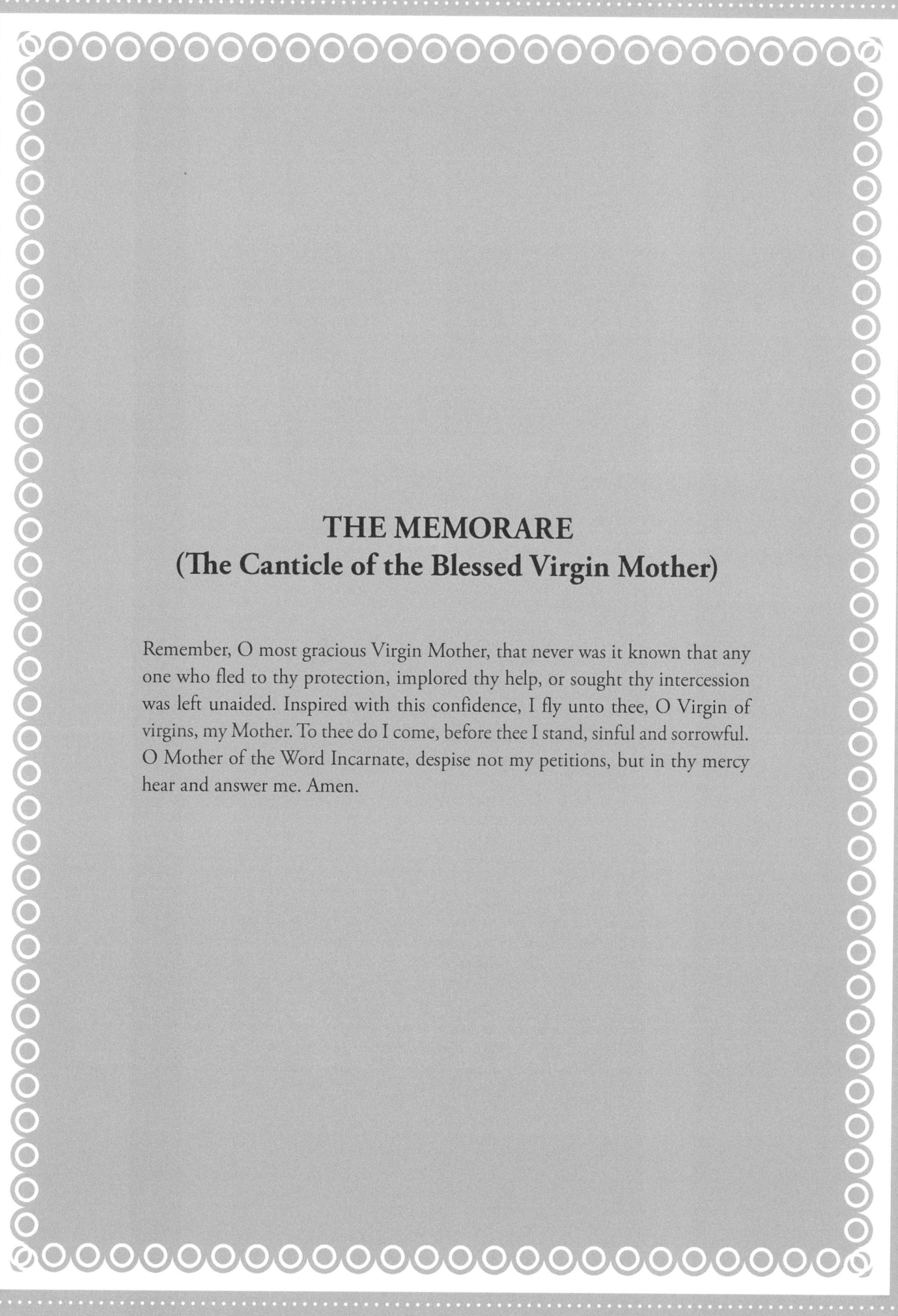

THE MEMORARE
(The Canticle of the Blessed Virgin Mother)

Remember, O most gracious Virgin Mother, that never was it known that any one who fled to thy protection, implored thy help, or sought thy intercession was left unaided. Inspired with this confidence, I fly unto thee, O Virgin of virgins, my Mother. To thee do I come, before thee I stand, sinful and sorrowful. O Mother of the Word Incarnate, despise not my petitions, but in thy mercy hear and answer me. Amen.

The colors of the night!

An early morning summer of 2010 memory!

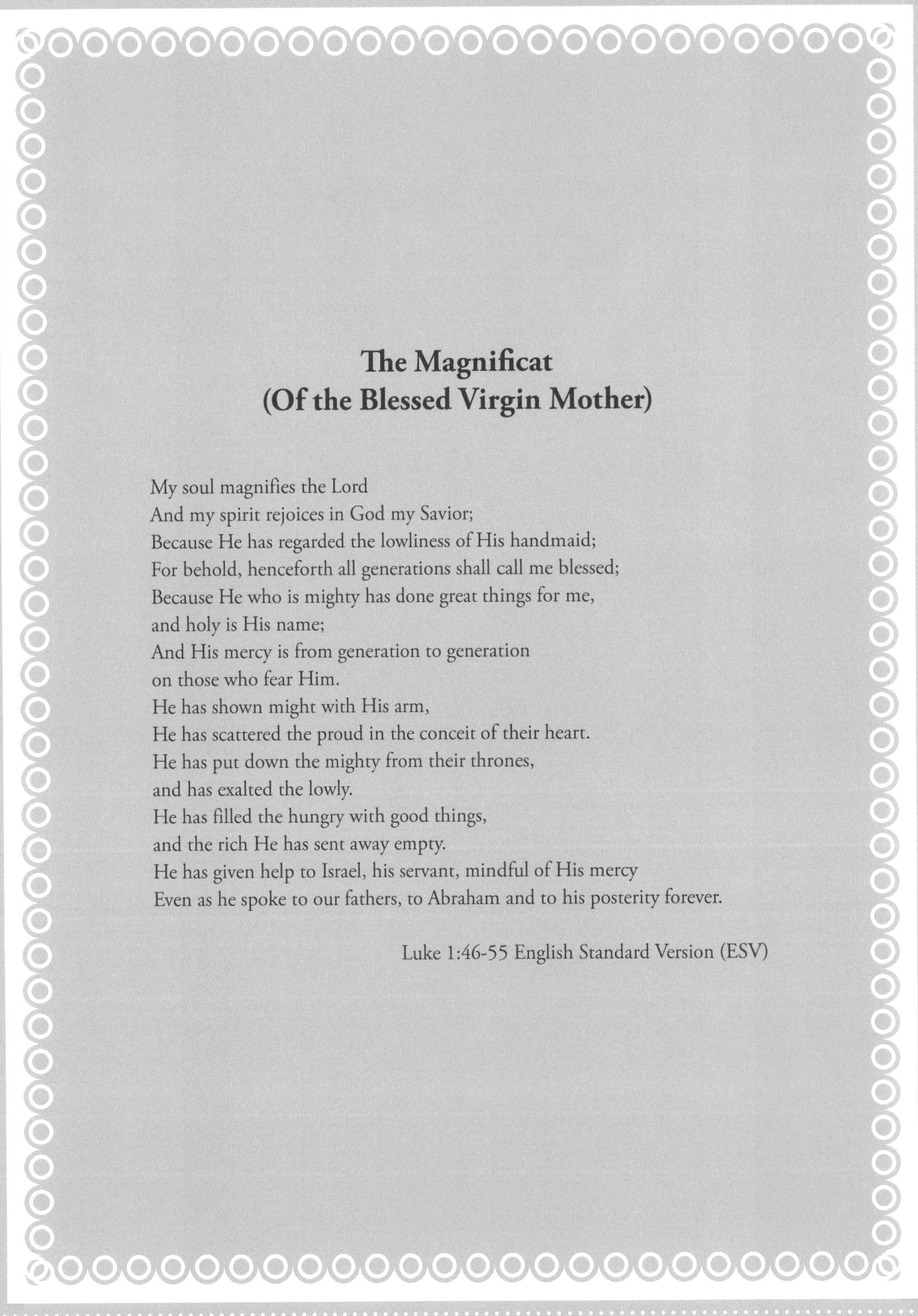

The Magnificat
(Of the Blessed Virgin Mother)

My soul magnifies the Lord

And my spirit rejoices in God my Savior;

Because He has regarded the lowliness of His handmaid;

For behold, henceforth all generations shall call me blessed;

Because He who is mighty has done great things for me,

and holy is His name;

And His mercy is from generation to generation

on those who fear Him.

He has shown might with His arm,

He has scattered the proud in the conceit of their heart.

He has put down the mighty from their thrones,

and has exalted the lowly.

He has filled the hungry with good things,

and the rich He has sent away empty.

He has given help to Israel, his servant, mindful of His mercy

Even as he spoke to our fathers, to Abraham and to his posterity forever.

Luke 1:46-55 English Standard Version (ESV)

Far from the maddening crowd.

Ripe SABA ready for cooking. Halina kayo at magluto tayo ng Maruya o Saba-Q! Siram!

To: Ms. Novett P. Mckenzie
(Belated Letter of Thanks)

We had always thought of writing you. Tomorrow come .t>morrow goe .md that tomorrow becomes today. Today, we found and have your address. So, there's no more excuse for not writing you today. Therefore thank God with humble heart for giving us today.

Yes, indeed.at times we get so caught up in our own lives that we unknowingly forgot to respond our hearts to those nice people around us who in their own simple ways did ordinary things in an extraordinary way, by touching lives of other people in their own special way. Looking backwhafs today without your help?

With this thought in mind, it is important that you receive the recognition and appreciation which you greatly deserved. Putting this on paper will help us get this message to you and the echoes it makes will make you a very special person for all those who knew you and the community at large.

We know you will never stop caring or making a difference-to touch other people's lives.   What you did to us during those most difficult times in our lives will be treasured in our hearts forever·. Again, thanks so much for everything. God bless..

With our warmest regards,
Frank & Mary Grace

Green Papaya was transformed into a work of art!

Advance Happy Thanksgiving to all my FB friends! Thanksgiving is just round the corner!

Viva la company!

Viva la company!

Dear Fr. Bob,

What an uplifting letter! Thank you very much for your every effort in writing to us. Your kind thoughts and prayers had helped us boosted our courage and strength to carry on - to face the challenge before us.

Mary Grace and I had always been a fighter ever since. When I lost my first wife of cancer in 1978 with three little ones, I could never imagine up to now how I struggled to survive with a mountain high of responsibilities.

With strong faith enfolding me, 1 believed that with God, there's nothing impossible to accomplish. In 1979, I found Mary Grace, a heaven sent to me.

We lived in New Jersey that time. We had a son named Francis. We lived in NJ till

1988. Then we moved to Palm Bay, Florida because we didn't like anymore the harshness of Winter in NJ.It was a big move leaving our good jobs behind.

Opening up a business was the only best idea that came to our mind during that time. So we opened up a Convenience Store at the corner of Eldron Blvd. and Jupiter St. We worked so hard night and day, seven days a week. At the end of the 5th year, our business never did good. We closed it down in 1993. All our investments were gone with the wind.

Just as we closed our store, Mary Grace got very sick. From the MRI results, it came out that she had a brain tumor as big as golf ball. The neurosurgeon told us that the surgery had to be done without delay. The following day she had the most delicate surgery done on her. On the course of surgery, she lost her optic nerve that made her vision impaired (legally blind), and also lost her pituitary and hypothalamus glands, the Master Glands of our body, the hormone-producing organs, like the endocrine gland, the thyroid gland, and the pancreas. In lieu of the natural hormones, she is taking steroids all along.

With no job, no money, and no resources to depend upon for almost two years, we struggled to survive with the Grace of God. I took care of MayGrace up to the time she could be on her feet. Because of the effects of the surgery, she cannot drive anymore nor get out of the house without me. How could we ever thank God for the many blessings He granted us? We cannot.

Again, thank you very much for your comforting and inspiring letter. We look forward to seeing you at Our Lady of Grace. Everyone missed you.

Best regards, Frank & Mary Grace

The latest picture of Frank & Grace at the Melbourne Square Mall. Things are getting greener on the other side of life. God is good all the time. To God Be The Glory Forever...

Rambutan (Tropical Fruit).

Work of Art in Autumn.

Freshly harvested Ripe Saba in the garden.

The "Banana Heart" - puso ng saging was born! Sarap man gulayin.

"Approaching Walt Disney World!"

On our way to Walt Disney World.

@ the Walt Disneyworld: EPCOT Center! Come one! Came all! Paradise is here!

A rustic garden floral arrangement - located in our patio.

Our Christmas Tree 2015 in front of our yard on the left side of the house. It's about 15ft. tall! I need some help to decorate this Christmas Tree!

My Green Haven!

Reserved for 13 guests at the Red Ginger Restaurant in Melbourne Square Mall. The hot & sour soup was good! (Y)

"From the Magic Kingdom With Love"

@ Main Street, USA

@ Walt Disney World, Orlando Florida

Long, hot summer dito sa amin! With my Australian cap, a souvenir from my sister-in-law, Ms. Roselli Gonzalo.

GOD BLESS AMERICA

God bless America
Land that I love
Stand beside her and guide her
Thru the night with a light from above
From the mountains, to the prairies
To the oceans white with foam
God bless America
My home, sweet home
God bless America
My home, sweet home.

AMERICA THE BEAUTIFUL

O beautiful for spacious skies,
For amber waves of grain,
For purple mountain majesties
Above the fruited plain! America!
America! God shed His grace on thee,
And crown thy good with brotherhood
From sea to shining sea!

Lightning Source UK Ltd.
Milton Keynes UK
UKHW052047110322
399897UK00002B/69